The
Secret Sauce
Book
of
THE HUNGRY MONK

written by
Kent Austin, Nigel and Susan Mackenzie
HUNGRY MONK PUBLICATIONS
Jevington Nr. Polegate, Sussex
Telephone: 032-12-2178

Sue
Mackenzie

Also in the same series:-

The Secrets of the Hungry Monk
The Deeper Secrets of the Hungry Monk
The Hungry Monk at Home

*We would like to thank M. et
Mme. Jo Bernard of the
Auberge du Vert for their
wonderful hospitality.*

**First published August 1982
Reprinted June 1985
Reprinted September 1990**

INTRODUCTION

No single word in the language of food covers such a multitude of sins and virtues as Sauce. Viewed by some with the deepest suspicion as a wily means of cloaking inferior food — worshipped by others as the heavenly lubrication that can transform the pleasure of eating.

Not unnaturally it is our view that the right sauce can have a profoundly positive effect upon the food it accompanies. Flavour is brought out rather than masked, complemented rather than fought, deepened to the point where nothing is left wanting.

To make such a sauce takes much skill and considerable experience.

In this, the fourth book in the 'Secrets' series we have attempted to distill all the experience that we have gained over fifteen years at The Hungry Monk and pass on to the reader a collection of sauce recipes that are both delicious and reliable. In most cases it is a reliability that has come from having found the simplest way of doing things — a factor that hopefully is common to all the Hungry Monk Cook Books.

The book is laid out around a series of 'Base' or foundation sauces that form the heart of nearly all sauces. So much of the 'mystery' of sauce lies in making these basics with painstaking care as it is here that so much of the final quality of a good sauce will lie.

Once you have mastered the base sauces it is a relatively simple matter to create not only the finished sauces that we give but an almost infinite number of variations. It is for this reason that we have allowed for two pints to be made of each base even though this is more than is required for most of the subsequent recipes.

N.A.M.

EQUIPMENT AND STORAGE

A word on equipment:- apart from a good whisk, a stout wooden spoon and possibly a Magimix food processor, it is essential to have a water bains-marie of some kind. This has two functions. The first is to provide a gentle heat for thickening delicate sauces. Bring the water to a point just short of boiling (180°F). The second is a means of keeping the sauce hot without it continuing to cook. For this purpose the water should be a little cooler (140°F). In these circumstances it is possible to prevent a skin forming by covering the surface with a piece of damp greaseproof paper.

On the matter of storage — most sauces will keep, and even improve, if kept in the fridge for a few days in a sealed container. But freezing should be approached with caution as the sauce may separate.

CONTENTS

BASE STOCKS AND ROUX

14

BASE STOCKS

FISH STOCK

This is a recipe for a base stock — however consideration should be given to its eventual use. Oily fish such as Halibut and Salmon are good for rich dishes. Cod, Plaice and Lemon Sole for plainer food.

INGREDIENTS FOR 2 PINTS/1.2 LITRES

4lbs/2 kilos fish trimmings (heads, tails and bones)
8 pints/5 litres of cold water
1 lb/450 grms. carrots
2 sticks of celery
1 onion
2 bay leaves
a few stalks of parsley
a level teaspoonful of black peppercorns

Method
Roughly chop the fish trimmings and vegetables. Tip all the ingredients into a large heavy based pan and bring to the boil uncovered. Simmer until the liquor is reduced by three quarters and allow to cool for a few minutes. Strain into a jug and leave until cold. Skim off any surface fat.

LIGHT STOCK

INGREDIENTS FOR 2 PINTS/1.2 LITRES.

3lbs/1½ kilos of Veal, Pork chops or Chicken bones
1lb/450 gms. of the trimmings
8 pts./5 litres of cold water
1lb/450 gms. of carrots
2 sticks of celery
2 onions
2 bay leaves
A level teaspoon of black peppercorns
Parsley

Method
Crack the larger bones. Roughly chop the trimmings and vegetables. Tip all the ingredients into a large heavy based pan and bring to the boil uncovered. Simmer until the liquor is reduced by three quarters and allow to cool for a few minutes. Strain into a jug and leave until cold. Skim off any surface fat.

BROWN STOCK

INGREDIENTS FOR 2 PINTS/1.2 LITRES

3lbs/1½ kilos Beef bones
1lb/450 gms Beef trimmings
4oz/100 gms Pork rind
8 pts/5 litres of cold water
2 sticks of celery
2 onions
2 bay leaves
1 level teaspoon of black peppercorns

Method

Crack the bones. Dice the pork rind. Roughly chop the trimmings and vegetables.

It is first necessary to brown the bones in a roasting tray together with the rind and a little water in a moderate oven. Then tip into a large heavy based pan together with the rest of the ingredients and bring to the boil. Simmer until the liquor is reduced by three quarters and allow to cool for a few minutes. Strain into a jug and leave until cold. Skim off any surface fat.

ROUX AND BLOCK ROUX

There are a number of sauces in this book, including the base sauces where it is much easier to make the roux as you go. However there are occasions when a block of ready-made roux can usefully be grated and whisked into a stock or sauce to thicken it.

Ingredients
Equal quantities of butter or margarine and plain white flour.

Method
Take a heavy-based saucepan and heat the butter until bubbling but not browned. Stir in the flour using a wooden spoon and continue stirring over a medium flame for about two minutes before proceeding with the particular sauce recipe you have chosen to make.

Block Roux
Remove the roux from the heat and whilst it is still warm, spoon it into an earthenware jar or bowl to set. Once set you can turn it out of the container and wrap it in greaseproof paper or foil to be kept in the refrigerator.

TRADITIONAL SAUCES TO ACCOMPANY ENGLISH FOOD

TRADITIONAL SAUCES TO ACCOMPANY ENGLISH FOOD

APPLE SAUCE
FOR PORK OR DUCK

INGREDIENTS FOR ½ PT/300ML

1lb/450grms cooking apples
2 tablespoons of water
1oz/25gms sugar
the juice of 1 lemon
a knob of butter

Method
Peel, core and slice the apples. The sauce is simply made by cooking the apple slices in a heavy based pan over a low heat with the butter, sugar, water and lemon juice. Stir occasionally. After 15 minutes the fruit should be cooked without being mushy. Transfer to a serving bowl.

BREAD SAUCE

For Roast Chicken, Turkey and Guinea Fowl

INGREDIENTS FOR ½PT/300ML

½pt/300ml milk
2oz/50gms fresh white breadcrumbs
1 small onion
1 bay leaf
2 cloves
2 tablespoons of white wine vinegar
a sprig of parsley
salt
freshly ground black pepper

Method
Firstly take the onion, peel it and make a clouté by pinning the bay leaf to it with the cloves. Next gently heat the milk with the onion clouté and continue cooking until the onion is soft. Top up the milk to the original level. Remove the onion and stir in the breadcrumbs, white wine vinegar and parsley. Simmer for at least 10 minutes, adjusting the seasoning as necessary. Remember this sauce is delicious served cold with leftovers so make plenty!

CUMBERLAND SAUCE

For Lamb, Cold Poultry, Ham, Game, and Terrines.

INGREDIENTS FOR ½ PT/300ML

¼ pt/150ml. Port
2 oranges
1 lemon
3 spring onions or shallots
3 heaped tablespoons of redcurrant jelly
1 tablespoon of French mustard
salt
freshly ground black pepper

Method
Take one of the oranges, remove the zest and cut into very fine strips. Squeeze the juice from the oranges and the lemon in to a small pan and bring to the boil. Finely chop the shallot and tip in to the pan to blanch. Tip in the remaining ingredients. Return briefly to the boil and decant in to a jug. Keep in a cool place but not the refrigerator.

FRESH CRANBERRY SAUCE

For Turkey and Game.

INGREDIENTS FOR APPROXIMATELY ½PT/300ML

1lb/450grms fresh cranberries
6oz/175grms sugar
¼pt/150ml water
The juice of an orange

Method
Wash the cranberries and boil them uncovered in a heavy
based saucepan with the water, sugar and orange juice.
Soon you will hear the berries bursting. Stir once or twice
and transfer to a serving bowl.

FRESH MINT SAUCE

For Lamb or Melon

INGREDIENTS FOR ½ PT/300ML

½ pt/300ml red wine vinegar
2oz/50gms fresh mint leaves
1oz/25gms castor sugar
the juice of one lemon

Method
Finely chop the mint leaves with the sugar. Mix in to the vinegar with the lemon juice and leave to stand for an hour.

GOOSEBERRY SAUCE

For Cold Mackerel - fresh or smoked

INGREDIENTS FOR APPROXIMATELY ½ PT/300ML
½ lb/225gms fresh gooseberries
1oz/25gms sugar
¼ pt/150ml water
the juice of one lemon
1 tablespoon of white wine vinegar

Method
Top and tail the gooseberries and boil them in an uncovered
heavy based pan with the water, sugar, lemon juice and
vinegar. Allow to simmer for a few minutes until the fruit is
soft. Transfer to a serving dish and allow to cool.

GRAVY

The secret to good gravy, quickly made, is to have a ready supply of roux (see page 18) in the fridge.

Once you have removed the joint and excess fat from the roasting tray, stir in some stock together with either red wine, brandy or sherry over a fierce flame, scraping the goodness from every corner of the pan.

All that remains is to introduce as much finely grated roux as you like your gravy thick.

Variation

One way to enhance the flavour is to roast the joint on a bed of finely chopped vegetables. These additional juices will of course be incorporated in the gravy.

HORSERADISH SAUCE

For Roast Beef, Smoked Trout and Mackerel

INGREDIENTS FOR APPROXIMATELY ½ PT/300ML

A stick of horseradish
1 fl.oz/30ml. of white vinegar
4oz/100gms fresh white breadcrumbs
¼ pt/150ml double cream
a dash of ready made mustard
5fl.oz/150ml of milk
salt
freshly ground black pepper

Preparation
Soak the breadcrumbs in the milk for 1 hour. Whip the cream.

Method
Scrub and peel the horseradish. Grate finely. Combine with the vinegar and mustard in a bowl. Take the breadcrumbs and squeeze out excess milk, before stirring in to the horseradish mixture. Fold in the whipped cream, season and transfer to a serving bowl and allow to stand for a short while so that the flavours develop.

SAUCES FOR MEAT, GAME AND POULTRY

SAUCES FOR MEAT, GAME AND POULTRY

ESPAGNOLE SAUCE

INGREDIENTS FOR 2 PINTS/1.2LITRES

3oz/75gms good dripping
2oz/50gms diced carrot
2oz/50gms diced onion
2oz/50gms diced celery
some mushroom stalks
1oz/25gms chopped fat bacon
3oz/75gms flour
2 large tablespoons of tomato puree
1 tablespoon of Worcestershire sauce
1 bay leaf
a bouquet garni
2½pts/1.5 litres of meat or vegetable stock

Method

Melt the dripping in a saucepan and fry the carrot, onion, celery, mushroom stalks and bacon until golden brown. Then tip in the flour and continue to cook for two or three minutes, stirring briskly. Gradually pour in the stock, together with the rest of the ingredients. Bring to the boil and simmer for 10 minutes. Adjust the seasoning and add gravy browning if necessary.

The next move is to reduce the sauce by about half a pint which can be done in two ways. Either rest a piece of greaseproof paper on the surface of the sauce and cook in a low oven for 1 hour, or if time is short, cook uncovered over a low flame for about half an hour.

Strain into a jug ready to use.

In the absence of Espagnole Sauce

We accept that there will be occasions when a cook might wish to produce some of the following sauces without being able to produce Espagnole first.

In the case of Shrewsbury Sauce, Port Wine Sauce and Green Peppercorn Sauce **only** it is possible to substitute a basic roux made with 1oz/25gms butter and 1oz/25gms flour brought to the boil with 1pt/600ml of brown stock and two tablespoons of tomato puree.

Alternatively 2oz/50gms of grated roux may be used.

We consider Espagnole Sauce to be essential for all the other sauces shown in this section if they are to have sufficient depth and interest of flavour.

APPLE SAGE AND CIDER SAUCE

For Roast Duck, Goose and Pork

INGREDIENTS FOR 1 PINT/600ML

¾pt/450ml Espagnole Sauce - see page 32
2 large cooking apples (peeled, cored and sliced)
¼pt/150ml dry cider
a large pinch of chopped fresh sage
the juice of two lemons
salt
freshly ground black pepper

Method
In one pan bring the Espagnole Sauce to the boil together
with the sage and lemon juice. In a separate pan poach the
apple slices in the cider. Combine all together and season to
taste.

BARBECUE SAUCE

For Pork, Duck and Kebabs

INGREDIENTS FOR 1 PINT/600 ML

¾pt/450ml Espagnole Sauce - see page 32
the juice of two lemons
1 tablespoon of ready made English mustard
2 tablespoons of mango chutney
1 large pinch of cayenne pepper or chili powder
salt

Method
Simply combine all the ingredients in a pan and bring gently
to the boil. Season to taste.

BLACK CHERRY SAUCE

For Roast Duck, Wild Duck and Goose

INGREDIENTS FOR 1 PINT/600ML

¾pt/450ml Espagnole Sauce · see page 32
12oz/350grms fresh or tinned dark or morello cherries · pitted
2 tablespoons of redcurrant jelly
the juice of a lemon
1 tablespoon of Worcestershire Sauce
1 tablespoon of French mustard
a dash of Tabasco
salt

Method
Combine all the ingredients and gently heat through,
simmering for 10 minutes over a low flame. Season to taste.

GREEN PEPPERCORN SAUCE

For Beef, Roast Pork, Fillet Steaks, Kebabs and Duck

INGREDIENTS FOR 1 PT/600ML

1pt/600ml Espagnole Sauce · see page 32
4 teaspoons of soft green peppercorns
the juice of two lemons
2 cloves of garlic
salt

Method
Crush the garlic with a little salt. Simply combine all the
ingredients in a pan and bring to the boil. Season to taste.

* See notes at the beginning of this section for an
  alternative way of making this sauce with brown stock and
  tomato puree should you not have any espagnole sauce to
  hand.

MUSHROOM BACON AND RED WINE SAUCE

For Fillet of Beef, Chicken, Guinea Fowl and Turkey

INGREDIENTS FOR JUST OVER 1 PINT/600ML

¾pt/450ml Espagnole Sauce - see page 32
12oz/350grms dark flat mushrooms
4oz/100grms smoked rindless bacon
1 onion
6oz/175grms fresh or tinned tomatoes
¼ pt/150ml strong red wine
1 tablespoon of vegetable oil
salt
freshly ground black pepper

Method

Wipe and quarter the mushrooms. Chop the tomatoes and the bacon. Finely slice the onion.

Lightly sauté the mushrooms, bacon and onion in the oil. Add the red wine and boil for a few minutes. Stir in the remaining ingredients and bring to the boil. Allow to simmer for 20 minutes, seasoning to taste.

This makes a delicious soup especially when served with croutons.

38

PORT WINE SAUCE

For all Game

INGREDIENTS FOR 1PT/600ML

¾pt/450ml Espagnole Sauce - see page 32
¼pt/150ml non-vintage Ruby Port
2 tablespoons of redcurrant jelly
1 lb/450gms of raw game giblets or trimmings
salt
freshly ground black pepper

Method
Firstly bring the espagnole sauce to the boil - add the giblets
and simmer for 30 minutes. Strain in to a separate pan.
Assuming that the game has been roasted, it greatly
enhances the flavour of the sauce to incorporate any meat
juices from the roasting pan. These can be combined with
the port and poured in to the espagnole sauce. Finally
spoon in the redcurrant jelly and simmer for a few minutes.
Season to taste.

* See notes at the beginning of this section for an
  alternative way of making this sauce with brown stock and
  tomato puree should you not have any espagnole sauce to
  hand.

SHREWSBURY SAUCE

For Lamb, Duck and Venison

INGREDIENTS FOR 1PT/600ML
Meat juices from roasting pan
1pt/600ml Espagnole Sauce - see page 32
¼pt/150ml non-vintage Ruby Port
2 heaped tablespoons of redcurrant jelly
1 heaped teaspoon of French mustard
the juice of a lemon
salt
freshly ground black pepper

Method
Assuming that this is being served with the roast meat, the sauce can be made in the roasting pan whilst the meat is kept warm on a serving dish. Pour off the fat and stir the port in to the meat juices. Bring sharply to the boil scraping the goodness from every corner of the pan. Spoon in the espagnole sauce, redcurrant jelly, mustard and lemon juice and heat through. Season to taste.

* See notes at the beginning of this section for an alternative way of making this sauce with brown stock and tomato pureé should you not have any Espagnole sauce to hand.

TURNIP SAUCE

For Duck, Wild Duck and Roast Pork

INGREDIENTS FOR 1PINT/600ML

¾pt/450ml Espagnole Sauce · see page 32
¼pt/150ml red wine
10 baby turnips (or larger turnips cut in to sticks)
12 button onions
salt
freshly ground black pepper

Method
The turnips and onions are best cooked in the roasting tray
with the pork or duck. Roast the meat in the usual way but
remove from the oven approximately 20 minutes before it is
fully cooked. Arrange the turnips and onions around the
meat, baste and return to the oven. Continue cooking
basting occasionally until the meat is done. Remove it from
the roasting tray and keep warm. Drain the fat from the
vegetables in the roasting tray, retaining the meat juices.
Pour in the red wine and bring to the boil over a strong
flame. Allow to simmer for 10 minutes. Lastly pour the
Espagnole sauce in to the liquor and stir gently, taking care
not to break up the vegetables. Cook for a minute until
heated through. Season to taste and serve with the meat.

CREAM SAUCES FOR FISH, POULTRY AND VEGETABLES

CREAM SAUCES FOR FISH, POULTRY AND VEGETABLES

VELOUTE SAUCE
INGREDIENTS FOR 2 PINTS/1.2LITRES

2pts/1.2l of light stock - see page 16 or fish stock - see page 15
2oz/50gms flour
2oz/50gms butter or margarine
salt
freshly ground black pepper

Method
Heat the stock gently. In a separate pan melt the butter before adding the flour to form a roux. Cook for 2 minutes stirring all the time. Gradually whisk in the stock a little at a time to form a smooth creamy sauce. Simmer for 5 minutes. Season to taste.

MUSHROOM PRAWN AND SOUR CREAM SAUCE

For Turkey, Chicken and Fish

INGREDIENTS FOR 1 PINT/600ML
½pt/300ml Béchamel Sauce · see page 51
8oz/225gms shelled cooked prawns
¼pt/150ml Velouté Sauce · see page 45
¼pt/150ml sour cream
8oz/225gms button mushrooms
half a green pepper
a knob of butter
a sprig of parsley
the juice of one lemon
salt
freshly ground black pepper

Method
There are three simple stages to making this sauce.

First wipe and slice the mushrooms and finely slice the green pepper. Fry in the butter until soft.

Secondly add the velouté, béchamel, sour cream and lemon juice and bring briefly to the boil

Finally just before serving stir in the prawns and allow to heat through. Season to taste. Chop the parsley and either add to the sauce or sprinkle over the serving.

FRESH CREAM FISH SAUCE

For poached or baked fish

INGREDIENTS FOR APPROXIMATELY ½PT/300ML

½pt/300ml double cream
3 tablespoons of fish stock · see page 15
2 egg yolks
the juice of a lemon
a little freshly grated nutmeg
salt
freshly ground black pepper

Method
This sauce is at its best the moment it is made and should not be pre-cooked as reheating is to be avoided.

To start, combine the cream, fish stock and egg yolks over a gentle heat, whisking continually, until the sauce achieves a thick and creamy consistency. On no account allow to boil. All that remains is to squeeze in the lemon juice, add the nutmeg and adjust the seasoning to taste.

WHITE SAUCES FOR FISH, VEGETABLES, POULTRY AND MEAT

WHITE SAUCES FOR FISH, VEGETABLES, POULTRY AND MEAT

BECHAMEL SAUCE

INGREDIENTS FOR 2 PINTS/1.2LITRES

2pts/1.2litres of milk
2oz/50gms flour
2oz/50gms butter or margarine
half an onion
1 bay leaf
2 cloves
salt
freshly ground black pepper

Method

Start by making an onion clouté - stud the peeled onion with the bay leaf and cloves. Bring this together with the milk to the boil in a heavy based uncovered pan. Simmer for 10 minutes and remove the clouté.

In a separate pan melt the butter before adding the flour to make a roux. Continue to cook for two minutes, stirring all the time. It is vital that a bechamel sauce should be absolutely smooth and the best way to achieve this is to pour the warm milk a little at a time on to the roux whisking vigorously until thick. Allow to simmer for no more than 5 minutes. Season to taste.

Lazy Man's Bechamel

For the hard pressed cook there is an altogether sneakier way of making Béchamel.

Method

Make a roux and drop it in to the cold milk with the bay leaf cloves and finely chopped onion. Place over a very low heat and virtually ignore save once in a while to give a quick whisk. Once it has boiled, season and pass through a strainer.

Amazingly this produces a beautiful creamy sauce whilst allowing the cook to do **all sorts** of other things.

CHEESE SAUCE

For Vegetables and White Fish

INGREDIENTS FOR 1PT/600MI

¾pt/450ml Bechamel Sauce - see page 51
5oz/150gms cheddar or gruyére cheese
1 teaspoon of English mustard
2 tablespoons of white wine vinegar
1 small onion
a knob of butter
a few sprigs of parsley
salt
freshly ground black pepper

Method
First chop the parsley and grate the cheese and onion.
Lightly sauté the latter in the butter until transparent before
stirring in the bechamel sauce, grated cheese, mustard and
vinegar. Bring gently to the boil whisking all the time. Fold
in the parsley just before serving. Season to taste.

CHESTNUT AND SHERRY SAUCE

For Beef or Venison

INGREDIENTS FOR 1PT/600MI

½pt/300ml Bechamel Sauce - see page 51
8fl.oz/240ml of double cream
a schooner of sherry
8oz/225gms chestnuts - peeled and roughly chopped
1 teaspoon of horseradish sauce
a pinch of tarragon
salt
freshly ground black pepper

Method
This sauce is best allowed to stand for 30 minutes or so before being eaten. This means that the meat juices should be drained off 30 minutes before the joint finishes cooking if they are to be incorporated.

Combine the meat juices with the sherry over a low heat. Toss in the roughly chopped chestnuts with the bechamel and horseradish sauces. Bring gently to the boil, fold in the cream and tarragon and simmer for about 10 minutes. Adjust the seasoning.

On those occasions when this sauce is to be served with fillet steak, medallions of venison and such like, a delicious alternative is to spread a thin layer of warm unsweetened chestnut puree over the top of the meat rather than including chestnuts in the sauce itself.

EGG, CREAM AND PARSLEY SAUCE

For Fish, Ham and Vegetables.

INGREDIENTS FOR 1PT/600ML

½pt/300ml Bechamel sauce - see page 51
¾pt/150ml double cream
⅛pt/75ml fish stock - see page 15 (light stock if serving with
vegetables instead of fish - see page 16
4 eggs.
the juice of two lemons
a sprig of parsley
salt
freshly ground black pepper

Method
Hard boil the eggs and immerse them in cold water before
peeling. Pass through a sieve. Chop the parsley.

The béchamel should be brought gently to the boil whisking
in the fish stock, lemon and double cream. Stir in the sieved
egg and chopped parsley and adjust the seasoning.

MUSTARD SAUCE

For Chicken, Cheese Soufflé, Turkey Breast and Ham.

INGREDIENTS FOR 1PT/600ML

½pt/300ml Bechamel Sauce - see page 51
1 heaped tablespoon of Moutard de Meaux
the juice of two lemons
¾pt/150ml double cream
1 tablespoon of white wine vinegar
a sprig of parsley
salt

Method
First chop the parsley. The sauce is simply made by combining the ingredients over a low heat in the following order:-
The mustard, lemon juice and vinegar, followed by the béchamel. Bring gently to the boil before finishing with the cream and allowing to simmer for a few minutes. Add the chopped parsley and correct the seasoning if necessary.

MAYONNAISE FOR SALADS, COLD SEAFOOD AND FISH

MAYONNAISE FOR SALADS, COLD SEAFOOD AND FISH

MAYONNAISE

This recipe produces a delicious plain mayonnaise that is in itself full of flavour and quite suitable with any salad, cold fish or cold meat.

INGREDIENTS FOR 1 PINT/600ML

1 pint/600ml pure vegetable oil
2 egg yolks
the juice of two lemons
1 tablespoon of ready made mustard
½ teaspoon of freshly ground black pepper
½ teaspoon of salt

Method

In cold weather take a double saucepan and warm the oil to blood heat. Place the egg yolks in a mixing bowl and blend in the mustard together with a little salt and pepper. It is necessary to alternately beat in small quantities of the oil until the mixture becomes very thick and then thin it down with the lemon juice. Continue this process, maintaining an even consistency until all the oil has been absorbed. The final consistency is a matter of taste and can simply be regulated by adding larger or smaller amounts of lemon juice. Adjust the seasoning.

The mayonnaise will keep indefinitely if kept in a properly sterilised air-tight jar.

If the Mayonnaise separates:- Stop! There is nothing for it but to start all over again with clean dry utensils. Separate an egg and place the yolk in a bowl. Pour on the broken mayonnaise mixture in a very fine stream whisking continuously. Once it has begun to emulsify the stream can be accelerated.

AILOLI

For Seafood, Cold Fish and as a Dip for Raw Vegetables

INGREDIENTS FOR 1PT/600ML

1pt/600ml home made mayonnaise - see page 59
2 gloves of garlic

Method
Crush the garlic with a little salt and whisk in to the
mayonnaise. It is a good idea to taste at this stage as garlic
varies enormously in strength and you may decide to
increase the number of cloves. There is nothing drearier than
half-hearted Ailoli!

Allow the Ailoli to stand for at least ½ hour before serving
to ensure a fully developed flavour.

CHILLI MAYONNAISE

For Shellfish or a Dip for Raw Vegetables

INGREDIENTS FOR 1PT/600MI

¾pt/450ml home made mayonnaise - see page 59
the juice of one lemon
1 chilli (fresh or dried)
half a small onion
1 cooked red pimento (fresh or tinned)
1 teaspoon of ground paprika
salt

Method
This is ideally made in an electric blender. Once you have removed the seeds from the chilli blend it with the cooked pimento, raw onion, paprika and lemon juice in to a smooth paste. Whisk this in to the mayonnaise and adjust the seasoning.

Allow this mayonnaise to stand for at least ½ hour before serving to ensure that the flavours blend and develop.

GARDEN MAYONNAISE

For Salmon, Salmon Trout, Hard boiled eggs and Salad

INGREDIENTS FOR 1PT/600ML

½pt/300ml home made mayonnaise · see page 59
a sprig of parsley
a sprig of mint
a sprig of lemon thyme
a small bunch of chives
the skin of ¼ of a cucumber
1 large pinch of powdered saffron
¼pt/150ml double cream
¼pt/150ml natural yoghurt
salt
freshly ground black pepper

Method
We are aiming here for a creamy mousse-like consistency.

Very finely chop all the herbs and cucumber skin.

Whip the cream until stiff.

Blend the mayonnaise and yoghurt, stir in the herbs and saffron. Finally fold in the whipped cream. Adjust the seasoning.

Allow this mayonnaise to stand for at least ½ hour before serving to ensure that all the flavours blend and develop.

GREEN MAYONNAISE

For Salmon, Salmon Trout and Hard boiled eggs.

INGREDIENTS FOR 1PT/600ML

¾pt/450ml home made mayonnaise - see page 59
a small bunch of watercress
a few young spinach leaves
a few sprigs of parsley
a sprig of tarragon
the juice of one lemon
salt
freshly ground black pepper

Method
The idea is to make a dry purée of the watercress, spinach, parsley and tarragon so as not to render the mayonnaise too sloppy. Do this by first blanching and draining the green ingredients, squeezing them dry in a tea cloth before passing them through a sieve or liquidiser. This puree can be stirred in to the mayonnaise. Seasoning and lemon juice may be added according to taste.

Allow this mayonnaise to stand for at least ½ hour before serving to ensure that all flavours blend and develop.

BUTTER AND EGG SAUCES FOR MEAT, FISH AND VEGETABLES

BUTTER AND EGG SAUCES FOR MEAT, FISH AND VEGETABLES

HOLLANDAISE SAUCE

Although hollandaise is the base of all the sauces in this section it differs from the other hot base sauces in this book in that it is perfect on its own with almost any meat, fish or vegetable. It is particularly good with food cooked in pastry.

INGREDIENTS FOR ½ pt/300ml

8oz/200gms salted butter
the juice of two lemons
3 egg yolks
half a teaspoon of French mustard

Method

This is a simple method of making a light creamy hollandaise using lemon juice and mustard rather than the more traditional reduction of vinegar with a bay leaf.

Start by thoroughly melting the butter, taking care not to brown it at all.

Next combine the egg yolks, lemon juice and mustard in the top half of a double saucepan away from the heat. Then place over the heat and whisk until thick and smooth (not scrambled!)

Transfer this in to an earthenware mixing bowl ready for the melted butter to be poured on in a thin stream, whisking all the time. The finished article should be smooth, creamy and shining with no sign of separation. There should be no need for further seasoning. Set aside keeping the sauce at kitchen temperature. Serve as soon as possible.

If the sauce should separate:- Do not be dismayed! Simply return the mixture to the heat in a double saucepan and bring up to a temperature hotter than blood heat but less than boiling. Take a clean bowl and fill it with boiling water —

this warms the bowl. Pour off the hot water leaving a teaspoonful in the bottom. Now simply pour the separated hollandaise in a very fine stream on to the water whisking continuously. There are other methods of retrieving hollandaise but this way is fool proof.

To reheat leftover sauce:- Follow the instructions above.

BEARNAISE SAUCE

For Steaks, Chicken and Fish

INGREDIENTS FOR ½PT/300ML
8oz/225gms salted butter
the juice of two lemons
4 fl oz/12ml dry white wine or dry sherry
3 egg yolks
1 shallot
1 teaspoon of black peppercorns
a sprig of fresh tarragon

Method
Finely chop the shallot. Boil the lemon juice and the wine together with the tarragon, peppercorns and shallot until reduced by half. This now becomes the basis when strained for the bearnaise. Transfer to a bains-marie, return to a low heat and blend in the egg yolks with a whisk, continuing until the mixture becomes thick and slightly foaming. Remove from the heat as it is crucial not to overcook at this stage. We are now ready to introduce the melted butter. This should be done by pouring it in as a thin stream, whisking vigorously. You will notice a white residue at the bottom of the butter - let this go in to the bearnaise. There should be no need for further seasoning. Set aside, keeping the sauce at kitchen temperature. Serve as soon as possible.

* If the sauce should separate follow the instructions on page 67.

CHANTILLY SAUCE

Beaten egg white makes this the lightest variation on
Hollandaise — For Fish and Mousseline of fish.

INGREDIENTS FOR ¾PT/450ML

½pt/300ml Hollandaise Sauce · see page 67
¾pt/150ml double cream
1 egg white
salt
freshly ground black pepper

Method
Whip the egg white until stiff and set aside. In a separate bowl
beat the cream until thick. Gently fold the cream in to the
hollandaise sauce followed by the egg white as deftly as
possible to avoid losing the air created for this sauce. Adjust
the seasoning to taste.

CHORON SAUCE

For Chicken, Fish and Vegetables

INGREDIENTS FOR ½ PT/300ML

½ pt/300ml Bearnaise Sauce - see page 69
**2 heaped tablespoons of peeled, seeded and chopped
tomatoes.**
salt
freshly ground black pepper

Method
Simply fold the prepared tomatoes in to the bearnaise and
adjust the seasoning to taste.

COLBERT SAUCE

For Steak or Fillet of Beef

INGREDIENTS FOR ½ PT/300ML

½ pt/300ml Bearnaise Sauce - see page 69
2 tablespoons of meat glaze

Method
Simply stir the meat glaze into the bearnaise and serve.

MOUSSELINE SAUCE

For Fish · Less buttery and therefore less rich than Hollandaise.

INGREDIENTS FOR 1PT/600ML

8oz/225gms salted butter
6 egg yolks
½pt/300ml of fish stock · see page 15
½pt/150ml double cream
the juice of a lemon
salt
freshly ground black pepper

Method
Boil the fish stock until it has reduced by half. Leave to cool. Meanwhile melt the butter completely. Transfer to a jug and keep warm. In a double saucepan gently heat the lemon juice, egg yolks, fish stock and double cream, whisking continuously. Once this has thickened remove the top half of the saucepan without delay and transfer the mixture in to a cold bowl. Take the heated melted butter and pour in a very fine stream on to the egg mixture, whisking all the time. Season to taste. You will achieve a thick creamy sauce that uses much less butter than hollandaise.

MISCELLANEOUS SAUCES

MISCELLANEOUS SAUCES

APPLE AND CALVADOS SAUCE

For Pheasant, Guinea Fowl and Pork.

INGREDIENTS FOR APPROXIMATELY ½ PT/300ML

½ pt/300ml double cream
1 good cooking apple
1 small onion
a knob of butter
a large measure of Calvados
a sprig of fresh sage
salt
freshly ground black pepper

Method
First finely chop the onion and the sage. Peel, core and
slice the cooking apple. Using the butter, sauté the onion
with the sage. Turning our attention to the roasting tray —
remove the meat once it is cooked and keep warm. Drain off
the surface fat and flambé the remaining meat juices with
the Calvados. Tip in the apple slices and cook for a few
moments — we do not want these to become mushy —
before introducing the cream. Turn down the heat and gently
stir, taking care that the cream at no time boils. The sauce
will gradually become thick and creamy and should be
served without delay.

PEPPER SAUCE

For Steak

INGREDIENTS FOR APPROXIMATELY ½PT/300ML (Sufficient for 4 Steaks)

½pt/300ml double cream
1 large measure of brandy
4 teaspoons of black peppercorns
a pinch of soft green peppercorns (optional)
a small clove of garlic
a sprig of parsley
salt

Method

There are various ways of making this sauce depending on personal taste.We favour coating the steaks with the crushed black peppercorns. These can be crushed in a coffee grinder or with the side of a heavy knife or even a pestle and mortar. Crush the garlic and chop the parsley.

Once the steaks have been fried remove to a warm place and drain any excess fat from the pan. The next move is to flambé the garlic in the brandy before tipping in the remaining ingredients. We consider the green peppercorns an optional ingredient — they certainly have an aromatic quality not to be found in their dried counterpart.

Taking care not to boil, whisk the double cream continuously until the sauce becomes thick and creamy. Pour over the steaks immediately before serving.

PROVENCALE SAUCE

For Seafood, Poultry, Steaks and Veal

INGREDIENTS FOR 1 PINT/600ML

1 lb/450gms peeled tomatoes (fresh or tinned)
1 Spanish onion
1 glass of dry white wine
2 fl.oz/60ml of olive oil
2 cloves of garlic
a sprig of fresh thyme
a sprig of fresh rosemary
salt
freshly ground black pepper

Method
Peel and slice the onion. Roughly chop the tomatoes. Crush the garlic with a little salt. Sauté the onions and garlic in the oil until transparent. Toss in the herbs followed by the wine and bring briefly to the boil. Finally add the tomatoes and season. Simmer for 15 minutes.

You don't have to be religious to work here but it helps

SATI SAUCE

For Spare Ribs, Kebabs and as a Dip

INGREDIENTS FOR APPROXIMATELY ½ PT/300ML

8oz/25gms Peanut butter
¼ pt/150ml of water
1 small onion
6 tablespoons of Soy Sauce
2 tablespoons of olive oil
1 tablespoon of tomato puree
the juice of two lemons
3 cardamon pods
1 clove of garlic
1 large pinch of chilli powder or cayenne pepper
salt

Method
Crush the garlic with a little salt. Pound the cardamon pods discarding the outer shell and grate the onion. These three ingredients are then fried in the olive oil for a few minutes. Now introduce all the remaining ingredients. Stir thoroughly and leave to simmer for 5 minutes.

This sauce can equally well be made with 8oz/225gms of roasted peanuts blended in a liquidiser.

SAUCE FOR SNAILS

INGREDIENTS FOR ½ PT/300ML

⅓ pt /200ml brown stock - see page 17
¼ oz/6gms butter ⎱
¼ oz/6gms flour ⎰ or ½ oz/12gms grated roux
4 oz/100gms butter
1 teaspoon of tomato puree
3 cloves of garlic
2 oz/50gms anchovy fillets
1 onion
1 teaspoon of ready-made English mustard
¼ pt/150ml red wine
the juice of two lemons
1 bay leaf
salt
freshly ground black pepper

Method
Start by thickening the stock either using the grated roux or melting the ¼ oz/6gms butter in a pan and using the flour to form a roux. Add the tomato purée and whisk over a gentle heat until thick. Decant in to a jug and set aside.

Now purée the anchovies, garlic and onion. Sauté in the 4oz/100gms butter for a few moments before stirring in the mustard, red wine and lemon juice. Bring to the boil adding the thickened stock and bay leaf. Simmer for 15 minutes, seasoning to taste.

An alternative method is to replace the thickened stock with ¼ pt/150ml of Espagnole Sauce - see page 32.

SWEET AND SOUR ORANGE JELLY

For Poultry, Lamb and Ham

INGREDIENTS FOR ½ PT/300ML

3 oranges
1 lemon
1 small onion
2 heaped tablespoons of redcurrant jelly
2½ fl.oz/75ml dry sherry
2½ fl.oz/75ml red wine vinegar
¼ oz/6gms powdered gelatine or 1 leaf of gelatine
1 clove
a dash of tabasco
salt

Method
Firstly grate the onion. Take one of the oranges and the
lemon and remove the zest to cut in to very fine strips.
Squeeze the juice from these two but cut the remaining two
oranges in to peeled segments. Next put the gelatine in to
the sherry to soften. Now combine together in a pan over a
low heat the grated onion, tabasco, red wine vinegar, fruit
juice and clove and bring briefly to the boil and simmer until
the onion is transparent. All that remains is to pour in the
gelatine/sherry mixture together with the redcurrant jelly,
orange segments and zest. Season to taste, check that all
the gelatine has dissolved and transfer to a serving dish to
cool and set.

NOTES

NOTES